MW01147688

THOUGHTS ON THE
SUZUKI PIANO SCHOOL

ABOUT SUZUKI™

HARUKO KATAOKA

THOUGHTS ON THE SUZUKI PIANO SCHOOL

A SUZUKI METHOD SYMPOSIUM
Translated by Kyoko Selden

Suzuki Method International, Princeton, New Jersey

CONTENTS

ABOUT SUZUKI is a series of publications dealing with the philosophy of early childhood education developed by Shinichi Suzuki. Beginning with the successful "mother tongue" approach to the teaching of violin and musicianship to very young children, his methodology has been expanded to include cello, viola, string ensemble, piano and flute. The Suzuki emphasis on teaching the whole child in the way most natural to each child has gained worldwide acceptance. Suzuki teachers can be found in every corner of the globe, and educators have become increasingly interested in comparing the Suzuki approach to other pioneering trends in childhood education. "About Suzuki" publications make the exciting and thought-provoking concepts of this international forum equally accessible to educators, parents, students, and the general reader.

HARUKO KATAOKA is one of the world's leading authorities on the Suzuki Piano School. Through her teaching and her personal trips to the United States and Canada, she has spread the message of Shinichi Suzuki that children can learn to play more naturally and with better tone. Born in 1927 in Tokyo, Kataoka began her study of the piano at age 6, studying with Yoshimune Hirata until she was 16. After World War II, she continued her studies with Haruko Fujita. In 1955, she was first introduced to The Suzuki Method. She travelled to Matsumoto in 1956 to study with Dr. Suzuki, and was deeply impressed with the results he was achieving in teaching children to play the violin. Dr. Suzuki's method not only affected her teaching, but also her own playing of the piano. Today, Haruko Kataoka participates in conferences, workshops, and summer institutes throughout the world on the Suzuki Piano School.

INTRODUCTION

What is The Suzuki Method?

THE SUZUKI METHOD is based on *the mother tongue approach.*

All human beings on earth at birth start to learn speaking their native tongue. I am sure you understand this. Nobody has felt "This is difficult" or "I hate it" in the course of arriving at language proficiency. It seems nobody has given it up midway, either, thinking it impossible. We have lived without giving special thought to being able to speak one language as though it were a matter of fact. However, it is a wonderful fact. Consider learning another language. What hardship it involves! Therefore, being able to fluently speak the mother tongue is a wonderful ability, however much we may take it for granted. What is even more wonderful is that every human being on earth possesses this capability. Dr. Suzuki is a great man who woke to this wonderful reality.

The Suzuki Method treats all children as equals. Traditionally, when students learn something, their achievements are quickly judged. The teacher rewards the child who performs well, labelling him as "talented," while neglecting the "less-talented" child. In other words, the result isn't the teacher's responsibility; it is up to the child to demonstrate talent.

However, when you think about it, this is very odd. If every child can learn to speak the native tongue, this would seem to indicate that all children have equal capabilities. Surely, if all children can learn to speak, they can learn to perform equally well in other areas, if their capabilities are properly fostered.

Some may think that the people of a country speak its language because they have inherited the ability, but the error is clear when we look at foreign children born and raised in Japan. They use correct Japanese with perfect freedom; they speak no differently than the Japanese. They can't have inherited the language as the Japanese might have. The same can be said of any country.

The method of learning, namely the method of fostering ability, is very important. If children are fostered by the same method as the one by which they learn to speak, any human ability can be developed whether in music or in academic fields. All human beings on earth are born with high potential for growth.

Dr. Suzuki realized this fact, and, since he was a violinist and educator, experimented with this method in violin teaching. Having achieved great success, he has been spreading the same approach to other areas, wishing happiness for all children on earth.

The Suzuki Method is based on Dr. Suzuki's profound love of humanity, of the personality of each individual. There are no human beings who are no good, who have limited capabilities. If there are any, it is because we have failed to foster their innate high potential. Shouldn't we think more carefully about how to foster them? Shouldn't we try fostering them by providing a similar learning environment as in the mother tongue? This should be the goal of all adults.

The Suzuki approach is not designed to foster professional musicians! Dr. Suzuki always says: "I am engaged in musical education for people other than professional musicians who occupy a tiny percentage of the world's population."

I think that at birth each human being is given a character by God or nature. I believe that this is what God has already decided, and human beings can do nothing about it. How one can make use of this gift from

God so that one can live in gratitude is the job assigned to humans. This means, in Dr. Suzuki's words, "Ability is not inborn; it is something to be fostered."

To foster during childhood diligence, patience, and ability to enjoy and delight; and moreover to foster wonderful human beings who can understand high art: This is The Suzuki Method. Naturally some will go into music, become scientists, or grow as politicians. Others will enter all kinds of other occupations. The Suzuki Method is an approach for fostering an individual so he will become a human being with fine ability.

My Introduction to The Suzuki Method

I was born in Tokyo in 1927. Since my mother was very fond of music, she started me on the piano when I was 6-years old. Of course, as there was no Suzuki Method, I was taught by the traditional method. Yet, fortunately, I was often exposed to good music and art, since my mother not only collected many records but was fond of going to concerts. In addition, as I was physically weak, my mother, wishing to help me live strongly by giving me rigorous training in a single activity, encouraged me to practice the piano 365 days a year without ever skipping a day.

The years of World War II were traumatic ones for me. When the war ended, I realized that I still loved the piano. I resolved to study the instrument under my own motivation. I first thought of getting a good teacher, and tried practicing as many hours as possible.

I was lucky to have a wonderful teacher, Haruko Fujita. She taught me a great deal, not only about music and piano techniques, but in other areas. I studied many pieces including Beethoven's and Chopin's concertos, Bach, Brahms, and Debussy. I frequently performed in concerts.

I studied awfully hard, putting my heart into it. I even tried 10 consecutive hours daily. However, instead of satisfactory performance, what I clearly felt was physical fatigue. A question arose: can it be that I am not suited to play the piano? In brief, I wasn't improving at all.

As I listened to great performers' recordings, I could hardly think that they agonized over their performances as I did. Instead, they sounded as if they were playing with great ease and enjoyment. Can something be wrong? After all I was not born gifted. I was no good! But why? I thought, don't I love music? Am I not crazy about the piano? I was about to fall into the abyss of disillusion. Then I heard Dr. Suzuki's lecture: "Talent is not inborn; everything depends on how it is fostered." Later I also read his books.

I felt as if I was awakened, and, wishing to study with Dr. Suzuki, I moved from Tokyo to Matsumoto. When I went to Matsumoto, Dr. Suzuki was convalescing for a year, unable to go out at all. Since I had already been teaching in Tokyo, Dr. Suzuki asked me to teach in Matsumoto. Matsumoto was still the country at that time. Few families owned pianos, and there were hardly any students.

My task was to accompany Dr. Suzuki's students while observing the lessons of the Suzuki class. In those days, he taught 12 or 13 junior and senior high school students, who later became outstanding performers or educators, as well as teacher trainee group lessons. This was a pleasant way to spend my days learning about The Suzuki Method.

Dr. Suzuki's younger sister Hina Aikawa was still alive then and cared for me. I visited the Suzukis nearly every day to be treated to food and to listen to Dr. Suzuki talk. Since this was my first encounter with him, I did not necessarily understand everything that was said; on looking back, however, I realize with fresh gratitude how many precious things he gave me during these first years to help me understand The Suzuki Method. I would like to share with others the happiness that I was given.

My Motivations for Writing this Booklet

For a long time I knew nothing about the world of music. Aside from the performances of the world's greatest artists and maestros with whom I was familiar through records and concerts, I only knew myself and my students.

In the past few years, I have had a number of occasions to visit other countries for the purpose of spreading The Suzuki Method, and to make contact with many teachers. I was a little surprised. I sensed that a greater number of people than I had thought may be suffering due to the traditional method of teaching music. I started to write this booklet, thinking that perhaps by writing, however clumsily, about my experiences, I could be of help to those unaware of this new method.

It is already 10 years since the Suzuki Piano School was started in the United States and Canada. Everyone understands that this is an educational approach which fosters children not through printed music but through listening. Children who were 5 or 6 when the method started are growing as wonderful, fine human beings.

However, coming into contact with teachers at workshops in various places, I am surprised by the many children who play with fingers curved too much while moving the wrists too much. Should we not play moving the hands more naturally? I would like them to play with greater attention to the tone rather than to the elbow, wrist, and hand shapes.

Dr. Suzuki is constantly studying tone in a thoroughgoing way. The quest springs from his deep love, which prompts him to ask how children can enjoy playing in the most relaxed way. Energy used differs completely between one who plays naturally and one who plays unnaturally with bad habits. In The Suzuki Method, children study tone and learn how to play with ease.

THE SUZUKI METHOD

THE SUZUKI METHOD is completely different from the traditional approach. Traditionally, elementary music texts are prepared on the basis of how adults think children learn. Beginner books first teach printed music. As for playing, they let the student start with whole notes which, adults believe, are theoretically the easiest to play.

Think how babies learn language. The first word or two may be simple. But after that they do not choose only to learn easy things. There is some reason in the logical theory that children learn things in order, starting with easier things and gradually learning harder things. However, human children are far more wonderful: Not being hindered by such logic, they simply absorb everything that is in their environment. Hence, it is most important to let children listen to music, that is, to create a good environment.

In The Suzuki Method, rather than first playing the piano, the important job is to listen to the music the child is trying to learn. Since starting The Suzuki Method in postwar Japan, Dr. Suzuki has demonstrated that "listening is essential." A good many people in different fields have understood this and are practicing it successfully. When one listens repeatedly, the music enters the mind; and the more thoroughly it is internalized, the easier it is to reproduce.

I, too, did not understand this well, but through experimenting with my own students, I can now confidently confirm that it is much easier and pleasanter to study when one listens than when one plays without listening. Take a look at how English is studied in Japanese schools. It is taught by reading printed texts and studying grammar, and is unsuccessful despite the many hours spent. Similarly, traditional music education, which teaches through printed music and music theory, cannot succeed (success meaning that everyone, not just some people, are able to handle the material).

Thus, Suzuki begins with the child listening to the music to be learned. For this, parental cooperation is absolutely essential (if not a parent, some adult). Babies grow through listening spontaneously to the voices of people talking around them from the time of their birth. Create a similar environment for your children. Never say, "I am playing this record for you"; just arrange it so that the music enters their ears before they realize it, spontaneously as in language.

Next, the child goes to the teacher for a lesson. The parent must accompany him. Children often forget what the teacher has said on the way home, even though they may understand it at the lesson. Therefore, adults should carefully listen to the teacher's instructions, and at home repeat them every day for one week, reminding the children of the assignment. With the same amount of time spent and the same amount of tuition paid, the result is surprisingly different between lessons attended by both parent and child, and those given to the child alone.

When people shop, they try to purchase good things as inexpensively as possible, yet when it comes to the matter of their children's education, they often throw away their money. This is probably because the results of education aren't immediately apparent. Dr. Suzuki always says: "Keep at it for 10 years: you will see the results well."

Babies cannot go on living if left alone. They must have grownups' help. At the beginning, piano lessons are also at the baby stage. Let me ask parents to give loving support without fail. Foster your child with love, although it may be a little hard. Don't you think that, from the viewpoint of your child's future life, this means giving him a wonderful present which cannot be bought with money?

Learning Can Be Smooth

As I already said, nobody learns the native tongue with pain. One masters it so naturally that it is hard to tell when and how one learned it. The way of learning in The Suzuki Method ought to be exactly the same as in the mother tongue. In actuality, it may be impossible, unless the child lives in a musician's home, to listen to music from morning till night in the same way as the child hears his native language.

I ask my students' parents: "It is good if your child listens to the piece he wants to learn 3 years ahead of time if possible; please let him listen longer than he practices the piano. The more he listens the better." When they listen a lot, children learn so fast that the teacher is surprised.

I say 3 years ahead of time simply judging from how much faster the younger one learns when siblings are studying. Starting now is fine. It's better to start now than to start tomorrow. If you haven't started your child listening to great music at an early age, you may think that it's too late, but there is no need to worry. Please start having your child listen.

Some may say, "Learning is easy? What a bad attitude! Learning is something that takes thinking and suffering!" The Suzuki Method, however, is a system for learning smoothly, becoming fond of wonderful music, and studying with enjoyment.

It is ideal, I think, to start feeding good music while the baby is still in the mother's tummy. As for starting to learn the piano, I think age 3 or 4 is best. In my view, earlier than that is a little hard. Unlike the violin, it is impossible to use an instrument which is adjusted to the size of the body (the piano is always the same size).

Why is earlier better? It is because childhood and adulthood are totally different. In childhood, one should be exposed as much as possible to the great works of art left by our predecessors, and absorb them with enjoyment. Later, passing puberty and entering adulthood, one must live by oneself on the basis of what one has acquired as a child.

When they see, hear, or face something, adults think with their minds. They are capable of distinguishing between good and evil. Naturally, children, too, can think; however, they receive everything through their intuition or senses before they do through their brains. They smoothly absorb whatever is there (whether good or bad).

Every adult was once a child; yet few adults remember what it was like when they were children. Please try to recall. Childhood is a wonderful stage where everything is possible. Don't waste your child's great period, but help him acquire wonderful, good music through The Suzuki Method.

Fostering Ability

In traditional music education, the teacher instructs children in a one-way approach. If a child progresses, he has talent, and if a child does not do well despite "good" teaching, he is no good! It is as simple as that.

The Suzuki Method is different. We instruct the child step by step to create ability. In actuality, the child first learns one piece by heart. When he has learned it very well, naturally he advances to the next piece. The same happens when he learns this piece thoroughly. However, what is different from the traditional method is that he continues to practice the former pieces constantly instead of forgetting them.

Try to recall how one learns language. When the baby learns a word, the delighted parents let him repeat it many times. When he learns another word, they let him repeat both words. For example, let's say that the child has learned to say "Good morning." Suppose the parents said, "Now let's learn the next expression," and no longer let him say "Good morning." If these parents were successful, a human being who could hardly talk would be created.

The Suzuki student must always repeatedly practice the former pieces! Teachers and parents who have never followed The Suzuki Method may respond: "Such a chore hardly seems possible." When you actually try it, however, it is very easy. Children not only remember the pieces quite well but, when they grow familiar with earlier pieces, the teacher will find it much simpler to instruct them to play them with better tone and more emotion.

At the stage where the child is just managing to play the notes, the ability to play the piece has not yet developed in him. Only when he can play a piece without having to think—i.e., without fear—is the ability to play it already cultivated. My Japanese is fluent and free from fears and errors, even when I talk in my sleep. This is because the ability to speak Japanese has been fully developed in me.

Let's think about language again. Do we teach newborns from letters? People would laugh at such an attempt. In The Suzuki Method, we never give the printed music to beginner children. Yet traditional music teaching has been doing this absurd thing with great seriousness.

How does the child learn music? By listening. If you play the Suzuki record once or twice a day, it is nothing for children to pick up and play the pieces in the piano curriculum Book 1 by ear.

By playing the pieces they have learned one by one, over and over, they learn to taste the joy of playing the piano fluently, taking delight in music. For children

raised on The Suzuki Method, there is no such thing as
what I was told long ago as a child at a music lesson:
"This piece is shaping up fairly well, so now start mem-
orizing it." Once they acquire the habit of learning the
sound through the ear instead of from the written notes,
children learn pieces so surprisingly fast that it would be
unthinkable under the traditional teaching method.

Ability is created through daily fostering. Those of us
taught by the traditional method have ability fostered
through seeing the printed music at every lesson, and
moreover through being commanded to memorize it as
if memorization were a separate job. All that was
accomplished by this was the growth of a troubling
ability to always perform, while worrying about whether
we may forget the next passage. In order to develop the
ability to play with absolute freedom, please be sure to
cultivate from the beginning the habit of playing without the music.

Music Should Be Fun

Music is something wonderful which enriches the
human heart whether with joy or with sorrow. Everyone
ought to have the right to cherish and enjoy music. Yet
people often say, "Music is too hard for me to understand; I don't like music." Why is this so? Since music is
created by great men, everyone on earth should be able
to enjoy it. Music is not a physical body called "music,"
but songs of the heart.

As proof of the fact that The Suzuki Method is a way of
learning which allows students to master the material
naturally and smoothly, all Suzuki students have grown
to be children who genuinely love music. This alone, I
think, is enough to let us call the method a great success.
Don't you think it wonderful that The Suzuki Method
will increase the number of people throughout the
world who enjoy listening to music and who understand
musical art of the highest standards?

HOW TO PLAY THE PIANO

The Beginner Stage is Crucial

TRADITIONAL common sense holds that it is all right if students do poorly at first, for they will eventually improve in gradual steps. Dr. Suzuki, however, considers the beginner stage the most important. If a wrong thing is repeated at the beginning, the ability to do the wrong thing (i.e., the ability to do poorly) develops.

What is inconvenient is that the human body always acquires ability that has been developed through repeated training, and when the person discovers that it is wrong, he cannot immediately discard it. Even if he understands mentally, the body is only capable of doing what has been assimilated through repetition. Therefore, as I think you already understand, what one should do is to accumulate what is proper from the beginning.

Do Human Beings Walk at Birth?

Have you ever thought about why human beings stand up and walk? Babies start to walk about 10 months after birth. It is a little wrong to think it a matter of course.

I, too, used to think it was natural that human beings walked standing erect. Then I read about the wolf children in Dr. Suzuki's writing. Abandoned in the Indian mountains and raised by wolves, they ran on all fours. One of them never learned to stand on her feet, even after months of training under human care.

When I came to know this fact, I realized that humans walked on two feet from infancy because they grow up seeing adults walk. This is exactly what The Suzuki Method is all about.

Is There a Child Who, After Starting to Walk, Becomes Gradually Poorer at Walking?

The answer is "No."

Nor does anyone stop walking.

Nor does anyone refuse to walk.

Nor does anyone become crippled unless by an unfortunate accident.

All people learn to walk before they know it, in a normal way, and so naturally that they don't even give it a thought. Moreover, they learn to move even more freely: They run; they dance. The explanation is simple. People around them are all walking beautifully.

Learning the Piano is Like Learning to Walk

Children should learn the piano just as they learn to walk, by emulating the adults around them. The best teacher is the one who delights us with wonderful performances. I am not talking about training professional performers, for I think the occupation of a performer requires extremely rigorous conditions.

But let's say that we love music and wish to enjoy playing the piano. This is a right that God has given everybody, I believe. It is truly sad and sacrilegious to waste this wonderful right. Then how can we avoid acquiring the skill to play poorly? Instructors must, I think, reflect on their own deficiencies and make efforts not to cripple their students' natural abilities.

Creating Ability

What struck me when I first came to Matsumoto was how totally different Dr. Suzuki's way of teaching was from that of traditional teachers, and how seriously he was studying one thing or another every day.

To confess, 28 years ago, I was myself a completely crippled pianist like a model of hopelessness. How did I correct this?

Dr. Suzuki constantly says, "One cannot correct ability. If one can do something, it is to triumph over the former poor ability by creating new ability."

Encouraged by these words, I tried accumulating ability through experimenting and studying new aspects of piano technique one by one. At first it was very hard, but when I mastered one thing, the next road opened up, and gradually I started to understand more. Still, I think it took me at least 10 years before I could change my way of playing. I am still studying. Maybe by age 80, I may be able to play naturally.

Once again, the beginner stage is truly crucial! Remember how ability is created! As you understand already, Talent Education is a method of teaching by creating a good environment, repeating and accumulating what is good and fostering ability for each child, instead of accumulating what is bad through repetition and ascribing the result to "a lack of ability by birth."

Learn one thing, patiently repeat it till it is sufficiently mastered, then proceed to the next. Patiently repeat both this and the earlier material. Ability is acquired in this way. Do not try to learn many pieces all at once. Instead, repeat every day what has already been learned without ever forgetting it. This is the crucial point for becoming able to play fluently.

When a beginner child studies Book 1, he starts out with "Twinkle" and learns the pieces one by one. We guide him in such a way that, when he has learned the "Musette" at the end of the book, he can fluently play all 17 pieces in the volume.

It is too bad that unison playing is not possible in piano as in string instruments. What the teacher can do, however, is to always listen to all of the pieces the beginner child has memorized. I have been teaching The Suzuki Method over a dozen years, and I know that this is something that any child can do with great ease.

Next, let's recall how important the initial experience is, how hard it is to correct the ability that is once fostered. Consider, therefore, how grave the first notes you teach ♪♪♪♪ ♪ ♪ are in relation to your student's piano playing for the rest of his life.

When one cannot play well despite great efforts, the reason is very simple. There is some place stiff and unnatural in the body; nothing more than that. This stiffness somewhere, I think, is already created at the very first lesson. The student who has acquired stiffness from the beginning rapidly accumulates ability to stiffen up. At college age, he may love music so much that he may wish to study music. He may enter music school and take lessons with a great musician, but he is in no condition to receive anything from him. Poor professor —but isn't the student even poorer?

Aren't there thousands of books in the world on piano technique? By the time we read those books, we are already grown, so it is too late. As long as we are in such a state as to be unable to play naturally, even if we understand mentally, the body cannot respond. We are hampered by the already accumulated poor ability, so that those books, however good, are quite useless.

That is why "Twinkle" at the very beginning becomes a crucial piece. In traditional teaching, the first lesson was not considered so essential. The traditional teacher believes skills gradually develop no matter what they are. Actually, skills must be taught properly from the first lesson.

Teachers in charge of beginner children: Don't teach them perfunctorily just because they are beginners, but rethink it as an important question that influences the entire life of each child. Study with fellow teachers, and try to foster the next generation beautifully!

CRUCIAL POINTS FOR INSTRUCTION OF THE BEGINNER

Listening

THE MOMENT we talk about piano lessons, both parent and child tend to think only about playing the piano. The Suzuki Method is different: listening precedes everything. Train your student to listen to the sound while he is playing. This applies to any instrument, not just to the piano. This is harder than you might imagine. In other instruments, you must find your own pitch, so it seems easier to create the habit of listening with your own ears. When playing the piano, it is easy to become insensitive, since all you do is play the instrument that's there. And what is awful is that, if you become advanced before acquiring the habit of listening, you turn into a person who can never listen to the sound you have actually produced. In short, the sound you have in your mind prevails.

Once, I was like that. About the time I moved to Matsumoto, tape recorders started to spread to general consumers. Since Dr. Suzuki emphasized tone so much at violin lessons, I bought a tape recorder and listened to my own piano sound. It was such a bad sound that it was a shock to me. The sound was completely different from what I had in mind. From that point on, I tried to listen carefully to my own sound with as much concentration as I could muster. A world of totally different sound opened up. Understanding your own sound is an important element for coming to understand others' (your students') sound.

Even with students who can play ♩♩♩♩ ♩ ♩ , I teach them to carefully listen at every lesson, so that they learn to clearly distinguish between bad and good tone. Whether beginners, intermediate, or advanced students, at each lesson I instruct them to be responsible for their own tone, and to recognize it as a mistake if they produce even a moderately bad tone, to concentrate, to listen, and to play with a selective mind.

As Dr. Suzuki always states, ability is something you develop through repetition. Unless you create good tone from the "Twinkle" stage, it becomes very hard later on.

Never allow the student to play haltingly. If you instruct the parents well so that they play the record frequently, this problem should never occur. The job of carefully and slowly practicing difficult sections becomes important later on.

Babies learn words little by little, but when 2- or 3-year olds speak, they don't speak at a very slow tempo. School English in Japan introduces students to language through printed letters, and lets them read at a very slow tempo. They may perform well on written tests, but cannot speak or enjoy English. The same can be said of the piano. Thinking that Book 1 is elementary so that students should play slowly is where the traditional method errs.

Dr. Suzuki always says: Children are much more wonderful than adults. If you ask them to play at a normal tempo (as on the record), every child can do it. If you let a child play stumblingly and repeat "Well done, well done," you are already fostering bad playing habits.

Tone

Twenty-eight years ago when I moved to Matsumoto wanting to learn The Suzuki Method, Dr. Suzuki once said: "Pianists simply pound on the piano with a big tone, but I wonder if beautiful, natural tone cannot be produced?" Since I had no doubt about the tone I was producing, I momentarily found his words strange. But somehow they remained in my heart. On looking back, I think that ever since I have been searching for the piano's tone, the natural tone.

The human body originally is made to move pliantly if alive. The piano keys are made to skillfully avoid the shock of collision by sinking about 1 centimeter (10 millimeters). However, if the student erroneously learns how to play by stiffening the body, the fingers and elbows rapidly grow stiffer every day through colliding with the piano, and in 10 years the student can no longer be corrected at all.

In the traditional method, too much care goes into the hand shape and elbow weight at the beginning. While it is certainly true that we play controlling the body weight and elbow weight, such exclusive emphasis only produces stiff and immobile fingers through putting the elbow weight directly on the fingers.

Care more about the tone than the shape. At the initial "Twinkle" stage, I always help produce a small and beautiful sound through moving fingertips naturally. You will notice that the sound produced thus is totally different from the sound produced through pounding on the keys with fingers curved stiff.

Some people misunderstand my emphasis on fingertips, and emphasize moving stiff fingers. This produces the same bad result as stiff and immovable fingers. Some even say that The Suzuki Method is a technique of piano playing with just the fingertips. Of course the piano is to be played with the entire body. It means to control the arms which are in a totally relaxed, desirable condition so as to achieve the best balance, and, to compare the fingers to walking legs, to walk deftly on the keyboard.

When you let the student produce a sound for the first time, ask him to get the finger "Ready," relaxed and unbent, and when he plays at the signal "Go," let him play with a small and beautiful sound by moving the fingertip very naturally. This is the important first step which hinders the student from losing the sense (intuition) of the fingertip. The student must always have fingers which can feel the weight of the keys with the tips. Let's try not to lose the delicate sensitivity of the fingertips.

Never Teach Too Much at a Single Lesson

I have a feeling that traditional teachers taught a lot at each lesson; so much that, after all, the student could absorb nothing.

Dr. Suzuki often talks of a "one-point lesson." During the lesson correct thoroughly just one thing which is the biggest problem, and instruct how to practice it for a week. When the student has accomplished one thing, add a next step to it. It is impossible to acquire many things all at once.

The traditional music teacher tells the student to "practice more" in order to make better progress. However, the teacher doesn't tell the student *how* to practice. When the student goes home, he hardly understands what to do in order to improve.

The parent can do nothing but say, "Practice." The child sits before the piano, plays the pieces he can play a few times, and has to go to the next lesson quite unenlightened as to whether he has improved. The parent, too, gradually comes to the point that he or she doesn't understand the situation, and eventually gives up, saying, "I don't understand music!"

When giving an assignment, you must instruct the parent and child how much the child should practice and what techniques need to be perfected. Let the student try during the lesson what you are going to assign. Always show the parent that the child can surely handle it, and ask them to repeatedly practice the assignment at home every day for a week. Isn't it the teacher's function to show the parent what the child should play and instruct parent and child in a concrete practice method?

At the beginning, the assignment includes only one point, so it is not such a chore for the parent and child, and they always do it. If the teacher says something difficult, or asks too many things, the parent who is no specialist in music will quickly start to say, "I don't understand" or "I am too busy to watch the practice." Instructing parents skillfully is also a very important point of The Suzuki Method. Since there is no parent who does not enjoy the child's improvement, please make it possible for the parent who understands no music to enjoy working with the child. In this, too, the beginning is really crucial.

Study the Technique of Piano Playing

The teacher need not be an accomplished pianist. For example, it is all right if the teacher cannot play a Tchaikovsky concerto. However, I would like him never to neglect the study of technique: how it is possible to produce a fine tone.

Adults can understand a verbal explanation of how to play the piano. However, the same is not true for a child. Music teachers too often try to verbally explain to children how to produce beautiful tone. Children spontaneously absorb what surrounds them through their senses and this precedes verbal communication. Thus, the student begins to sound exactly like the teacher who plays the piano sitting next to him. If the teacher can give a fine verbal explanation but plays with a miserable tone, the child will also play poorly. Over 20 years ago when I moved to Matsumoto and came into daily contact with Dr. Suzuki, I was struck by how, each time he found a spare moment, he studied what he could do to produce fine tone.

Written Music and Music Theory are Unnecessary

The Suzuki Method is the mother tongue approach. Do you teach letters to a newborn? You teach him how to read little by little after he has learned to speak fluently. It is the same thing for music. Children who start without printed music always think and enjoy music through the sound, much to my envy. (Of course they will learn reading, and will read perfectly later on.) Those who entered music through the written music have acquired the inconvenience of being unable to do anything unless they have the music.

As I have written before, those who study the piano ought to start to learn reading in The Suzuki Method much earlier than those studying melody instruments. The reason is that children who learn music through the sound may be slow at first, but soon start to advance very rapidly. When this happens, the parents become lost unless they can play the piano. Reading will prove useless in a practical sense, when taught separately from performance. It can be useful only when learned along with the body movement while playing, and within the context of the piece being played.

This is easy to understand if you think in terms of language. You cannot readily use a foreign language learned from books, but you can use a foreign language learned while living and acting in its culture.

Theory is totally unnecessary for small children. In the mother tongue, which one can learn to speak fluently from babyhood, no one seriously attempts to teach grammar to children. They spontaneously pick up grammar in the context of daily life. Don't you think it is the same with music? What the child has absorbed while learning and playing various pieces with enjoyment, and what he has absorbed from the teacher's occasional instructions, alone prove useful later on. The child can learn theory when he is over 10-years old, when he can play with sufficient skill, or even later. Dr. Suzuki always says that you can understand theory if you read books after growing up.

Learning through Repetition

Encourage your students to practice the pieces learned earlier. Let's think again about language. In language, we always use the words we have already learned; we never say we are through with them when we learn new words. For example, ever since learning to say "Good morning," we have used it every day. This is how we come to be able to speak fluently without making mistakes.

This is a very important point in The Suzuki Method. In the traditional method, the student practiced only the piece he was learning, and received lessons only on that piece. This was normal. The Suzuki Method is quite different: Repeated practice of former pieces is the basis for progress.

In a piece the student has just memorized and is playing with effort, all the attention goes to playing it. Even if the teacher gives good instructions, the child cannot take in anything. Since he is more relaxed about a familiar piece he has been playing for a long time, he can absorb the teacher's good instructions, and therefore gradually learns to play each piece with finer tone.

At a Book 1 student's lesson, therefore, I always listen without fail to all the pieces he can play. And starting from pieces that have become familiar, I try to correct weaknesses little by little. If the teacher does not listen at the lesson, both the student and parent begin to neglect practicing earlier pieces at home. Dr. Suzuki has recently invented what is called "the lottery concert." This approach involves cards with the names of pieces placed in a box. Children pick a card from the box, and must play the piece drawn.

In string and other instruments, conveniently, unison playing is possible, but the piano is a little hard in this respect. The teacher has to listen to each child individually. Even so, since review practice is very important, the teacher must help cultivate this habit at the Book 1 stage.

Learning from Other Students

Create the habit of listening to other students' lessons before leaving! This is not to tell students to compete with each other. The teacher should schedule lessons so that a student's lesson is followed by another child of about the same age studying a piece a little further ahead. This way, he can always watch a lesson on a piece he is going to study.

Human beings grow by learning from their environment. Therefore, we learn much more while observing how other people around us study: the same amount of study can have completely different results in growth. Through sharing each other's lessons, children can make friends in class. They can influence each other, help each other, and enjoy growing together. The time spent when watching another's lesson is part of one's own lesson.

Parental Assistance

As a baby cannot live alone, in piano lessons, too, good parental assistance is necessary at the beginning. Three- to 5-year olds cannot make plans. Therefore, the assistance of adults who can make plans is bound to be necessary. Every parent in the world, I think, wishes to bring up her own child better. It is vital for teachers to instruct parents well at the first lessons.

Unlike melody instruments, one has to play the piano with both hands skillfully harmonizing the solo and accompaniment parts. How can parents, the majority of whom know no music, help children learn a piece? The teacher must coach the parent during the Book 1 stage so that the approach is understood securely.

A new piece is not taught by the instructor during lesson time. The student learns new pieces by listening to the Suzuki records at home. Learning the new piece is a job the parent and child should complete together. When the child can play a new piece fairly well from memory, the teacher listens to it at the lesson. Therefore, first they have to learn the best way to prepare a new piece.

In each piece after "Twinkle" in Book 1, I have the child memorize just the right-hand part (which is easy for the parent and child who listen to the record) and listen to it at lesson. When the right hand is fluent, I let the child practice the left hand, then play both hands together. I explain to the parent: "Since Book 1 is beginner material, I give lessons on the right and left hands separately so that it is easy for you to understand. But when you advance to Book 2, I no longer separate them. Always learn to play with both hands together before bringing a piece to class." No matter how little music the parents know, if the teacher skillfully coaches them at the Book 1 stage, it is not difficult for parents to help their children learn the Book 2 pieces.

The First Lesson

I N THE SUZUKI METHOD, the teacher does not teach an individual student alone as in the traditional method. A group of students comes to lessons in the same time slot, and, instead of each leaving right away after his own lesson, everybody stays to listen to each other.

That is because it is often easier to recognize other people's mistakes than our own. Parents often understand instructions better when another's child is receiving them, than when their own children are being corrected. Children, too, can learn while enjoying each other. Therefore, when a new student-parent couple comes to study by The Suzuki Method, we clearly explain our approach, and tell the parent that, above everything else, it is of prime importance to listen to music.

If, as in my case, a classroom already exists, we ask them to come to observe lessons of Book 1 students. They observe at least two or three weekly lessons (in some cases over a period of 1 to 3 months) before actually starting. If you are starting a new class, it is recommended that you wait until you have two or three students and then start them together as a group.

Now, my first lesson consists of asking the student to stand before me face to face. I then ask him to follow my instruction: "Stand with your feet together"; "Put your hands neatly at your side"; etc. For a 3-year old, standing with his feet together is a fairly difficult job. If the child fails to do this, I ask his parents to have him practice it patiently at home, several times daily.

This is a very important lesson. As I said before, ability is created through repetition, so the first lesson is the first step toward creating ability to clearly understand and respond to what the teacher is saying. The law by which good ability is created is this: When one thing is accomplished, repeat it until it is thoroughly mastered, then learn the second thing. Learn it in the same way, and when fluent in both, go on to the third. Keep using the previous steps while you accumulate new capabilities.

If the child is capable of standing correctly, I teach him how to bow. When the student and I face each other and bow, the meaning behind it is respect for each other as two human beings rather than as teacher and pupil: "Let's greet each other in mutual respect and start the lesson." As long as the child cannot handle these two steps, I never let him sit before the piano.

As I already said, the beginning is crucial no matter what it is. If only the teacher and the parent guide and foster properly without forcing, every child can enjoy learning. Traditionally, too much was taught at once, whether at the beginner stage or later on, with the result that nothing developed well.

The Piano Stool

The grownup who can already play the piano well knows how to adjust the height of the piano stool. However, a child who is starting to play the piano should be helped to sit at such a height that he can properly balance his body. This is very important.

Let him sit first with his elbows at his sides. Bring the hands forward; detach the elbows a little from the body, and put the hands forward a little further. The keyboard should be right under the palms. Choose a stool that allows this height. Give instructions so that the child will sit on a stool meeting the same conditions at home. If the child is small, naturally his legs will not reach the floor. Prepare a foot stool (a simple wooden stool will do). Teach the parent how the child should sit.

"Getting Ready" to Play

When the child succeeds in sitting correctly on the stool, teach how to "get ready" with finger no. 1 (the thumb) on the note C: ♩ . Instruct the child to keep the thumb still on the key without moving the body (never let him make the sound). A 3-year old can hold his thumb steady for about 3 seconds at first. Some find it difficult to stay still even for 1 second. But there is no problem if the child cannot do it at first. Ability is something you develop: if you take time (take days) and have him practice steadily, every child comes to accomplish it. Wait until he can sit still for 10 seconds or so.

"Getting ready" is extremely important, for, if the child has learned to prepare well, when he becomes an advanced student playing difficult pieces, he can stay calm and play easily. What does the child learn through "getting ready"? Since this requires balance, the child learns to poise himself skillfully. It also serves as practice for developing concentration.

Children are good at moving. Except when they are asleep, they are almost always moving. It seems quite difficult for them to stay still. Therefore, don't take it lightly thinking it is easy for the child to hold his thumb still. Instruct the child to practice with his parent at home every day, no matter how many weeks it may take, until he can do it properly. (At first, the child learns to prepare with the right hand. After the right hand, let him learn to prepare in exactly the same way with the left hand.)

Adults often feel a lesson is unsatisfactory unless

some sound is being made on the piano. Practice in "getting ready" tends to be neglected. By learning to prepare, the student becomes good at balancing the body, and concentration also grows. Playing after getting ready and settled helps produce sound under good conditions. Moreover, if the habit of getting ready is thoroughly acquired, the student never plays on impulse, and it becomes very easy for the teacher to instruct him.

Beginning to Play

Now the child is ready to play ♪♪♪♪ ♪ ♩ (the 1st variation from the "Twinkle Variations" in the Suzuki Piano Book 1). The child practices playing with the first finger on the note C. At first, I hold the child's hand (his elbow with my left hand and his hand with my right hand). I say to the child, "Ready!" then, "Go!" With this signal we play the rhythm. I am holding the child's elbow and finger, so in fact I do the playing. We repeat this many times. The child spontaneously learns the rhythm while doing this.

So, the teacher has to take every caution to move the fingertip naturally, using a small tone. If the sounds ♪♪♪♪ ♪ ♩ are poor (stiff, or too loud), the child at this earliest stage learns that bad sounds are normal sounds. Use a natural sound. Think of the child's body; recall the baby's feet when walking for the first time. Play with a small and beautiful tone suitable to the small hand.

Always play after the commands "Ready" and "Go." After playing with the child, let him play by himself. If he can play in the same way, fine, but if not, let him try playing with your assistance again many times. Ask the parent to have him repeatedly practice this at home for one week, no matter how briefly each time. Of course he only plays the single figure ♪♪♪♪ ♪ ♩ on C with the first finger.

Here again, the question of ability is important. If you help him play 𝅘𝅥𝅯𝅘𝅥𝅯𝅘𝅥𝅯𝅘𝅥𝅯 𝅘𝅥𝅮 𝅘𝅥 easily with one finger, the rest of the "Twinkle" melody becomes more easily manageable. But, if the teacher hastens to teach the first, fourth, and fifth finger, the child may learn the order of the notes, but the whole thing, built on an imperfect rhythm of 𝅘𝅥𝅯𝅘𝅥𝅯𝅘𝅥𝅯𝅘𝅥𝅯 𝅘𝅥𝅮 𝅘𝅥 , will become a clumsy "Twinkle." If you cultivate high ability with the rhythm on a single note, the child can do the rest instantly at the same high level. As for the order of the notes (which adults find difficult to master), you needn't worry: There is no child who cannot memorize it as long as you play the record for him.

Whether it takes 2 weeks or 3 weeks, keep giving a lesson only on this one thing until the child accomplishes it. It may seem so simple to grownups, but a 3-year old who concentrates on facing the piano for the first time in his life makes no less effort to play 𝅘𝅥𝅯𝅘𝅥𝅯𝅘𝅥𝅯𝅘𝅥𝅯 𝅘𝅥𝅮 𝅘𝅥 than an advanced student does in playing a long piece.

When the student can play 𝅘𝅥𝅯𝅘𝅥𝅯𝅘𝅥𝅯𝅘𝅥𝅯 𝅘𝅥𝅮 𝅘𝅥 with the first finger, let him play the rhythm on G using the fourth finger. Always first practice getting ready, then play at the signal, "Go." He should be able to do this at once. Next, play the same on A with the fifth finger. As I have already written, the most important thing here is to practice playing securely at the signals, "Ready" and "Go."

When the student can play the First Variation 𝅘𝅥𝅯𝅘𝅥𝅯𝅘𝅥𝅯𝅘𝅥𝅯 𝅘𝅥𝅮 𝅘𝅥 skillfully, teach the Second Variation, 𝅘𝅥𝅮 𝅘𝅥 𝅘𝅥𝅮 . Follow the same steps as in the First Variation: "Ready," "Go," and play from the first finger. The teacher helps the child learn by holding his hand and elbow, and playing the rhythm with him.

What is difficult in 1 2 3 4 is to let 2 3 sing long. If, after hitting the key, the finger stays still on the key to make the note long, stiffness will result and interfere with free movement. Prepare the finger by keeping it straight at "Ready," play at "Go" making a motion as though to grab, then rock the finger that has played the note just slightly forward. It becomes easier to hold the long note this way.

Although this variation is hard because of the syncopation, since it is important, please teach it step by step as explained before, until it becomes secure.

Next, play ♩ ♫ ♩ ♫ , the Third Variation. Again practice this step by step from the first finger with the signals "Ready" and "Go." The way to play it easily is to play with a very small sound. After thorough practice in playing with the signals "Ready" and "Go" between rhythms, instruct the child to play the variation without stops. Even after becoming able to play without stopping after each rhythm, the student must not forget to practice with "Ready" and "Go." Always practice both ways.

Legato and Staccato

Legato and staccato should be taught when instructing the "Twinkle Variations." There are few problems if the teacher plays good legato and staccato for the child by his side. However, in the case of children who are apt to become tense, you must teach the two techniques carefully even if it takes a long time.

Legato is the most basic technique in piano playing. To compare it to human movement, it is like walking very naturally. We walk lightly by moving our two legs: We put them forward alternately, shifting the upper body smoothly and skillfully on the left or right leg. Think of the palm of the hand as the body, and the fingers of the hand as the legs. At the beginning, let the child move the fingers very naturally (as though walking with legs), minding what kind of tone is being produced rather than how the fingers are shaped.

The traditional method was too concerned about the shape of the hand and elbow at the early stage, making the child start out being stiff. The result was that it hampered movement. Who pays attention to the shape of the feet when a baby starts to walk? No one on earth gives heavy shoes to the baby just starting to walk. When the child can walk fairly naturally and skillfully, he will be able to learn skipping, dancing and many other variations.

The "Twinkle" theme includes many occasions in which the same note is repeated twice legato. Legato playing of the identical notes is difficult. Teach it very carefully. After "Twinkle," you find this in "Cuckoo," "Lightly Row," "French Children's Song," "Mary Had a Little Lamb," "Go Tell Aunt Rhody," "Clair de Lune," "Good-bye to Winter," "Allegro 1," and the first notes of "Musette."

"Little Playmates" includes many scales. It is very important to practice playing these scales in perfect legato without slipping. As a method of practice, let them play C D E F G using the rhythm ♫♫ ♪♩ for each note. After practicing this several times, have them play C D E F G legato. This helps keep them from slipping. Do the same exercise for both the right and the left hands.

"Allegretto 2" contains a unison scale. Teach it with great care. The left and right hands have to be in perfect unison. A good way to instruct this is to have the student play the section of the sixteenth notes in a very small tone.

Before discussing staccato, let's think about the rhythm which the student plays when starting to learn the piano by The Suzuki Method. I don't consider this to be staccato. A baby stands before walking. He cannot walk unless he learns to balance for standing. In the same way, I consider ♫♫ ♪♩ to be practice for learning what kind of balance the body, elbows, and fingers need in order to stand on the keyboard.

When a human being actually stands on the ground, the ground does not bend, so it is easy to understand how to balance in standing. However, when the child presses down on the piano keys with his fingers, the keys sink. Since the fingers are not the lowest part of the body as are the legs, it is a little difficult to understand the balance. It is easier for the child, therefore, to acquire the balance if the notes are detached ♩♩♩♩ ♩ ♩ in a non-legato way.

At the very beginning, these notes have to be played with a small tone without forcing anything. The teacher must be able to judge the balance of the student's body. When the balance is poor, the student can never produce a good sound. Every student gradually develops while learning pieces. You must guide him so that by the time he plays "Allegro 1" toward the end of the book, he can play correct staccato, not non-legato.

Now we're ready to play the Fourth Variation of "Twinkle," the legato theme. The legato passages of the same notes are difficult for the pianist. Please teach your students with care until they can play with perfect legato. First teach C C at the beginning. Try to recall the Second Variation. Play the first C note in the same way as the long note 2 3 in 1 2 3 4 in this variation. Instead of holding the fingers and palm stiff, play the note singingly, as though lifting the hand slightly forward. When this one note is played well, all you do is repeat it once more.

Many students accomplish the legato playing of these two identical notes after 1 week of homework. Then teach playing C and G legato, connecting the first finger (C) to the fourth finger (G). Keep at it until the student accomplishes it, whether it takes 1 or 2 weeks. Never try to let the student play the entire melody during the lesson while his basic technique is still imperfect.

Once the legato of the first three notes, C C G, is learned, the rest is simple. Thanks to the teacher's good guidance, the student should have been listening to the record, and the melody is very much in his mind. He can now readily play the whole piece.

How to Study

When the child has learned to play "Twinkle" skillfully with the right and left hand separately, he advances to the next piece. My method is to let the student first learn the melody with just the right hand. If the teacher is doing a good job in instructing, the parents are playing the record at home every day, and the students have also already learned how to do legato acceptably. Therefore, if the teacher says, "Memorize the next piece by the next lesson," both parent and child are happy to do so.

In such pieces as "London Bridge" and "Go Tell Aunt Rhody," which contain difficult fingerings, prepare the parent carefully when assigning the piece so that there will be no mistakes. If the student learns the piece with the wrong fingering, it is a chore to correct it later. I have a feeling that this is another proof of the human habit of never forgetting what was learned at the beginning.

After the student has learned the right hand of nearly all Book 1 pieces (half is also fine), we begin study of the left hand. First teach the parent how to practice the left hand of "Cuckoo," and ask the child to repeatedly practice and memorize it at home. This suffices for some children: They bring the completed piece to the next lesson with both hands put together. Focusing on "Cuckoo," I carefully teach the parent at the lesson how to put both hands together:

1. "Get Ready." When the child is told to get "Ready," both hands have to be ready at once with the right hand fifth finger on G, and the left hand fifth finger on C.

Repeat this until the student can do it.

2. When both hands can be ready on the first notes without hesitation when told to be "Ready," say "Go," and let the child play the right hand G and left hand C together. Repeat it many times.

3. When the child can do this, let him play, while still listening to the G sound of the right hand, the E sound with the left hand's third finger. Since this is a little difficult, repeat it slowly.

4. Next, put together the right hand third finger on E and the left hand first finger on G.

When you teach just these processes and ask the child to practice this much at home for a week, nearly all children can play the entire song of "Cuckoo" at the next lesson using both hands. Thus, we have taught the parent how to guide the child to learn to play a piece with both hands. Therefore, from the next piece on, they can work together on their own at home: First the left hand and then both hands.

The Suzuki Method is an approach by which the child learns little by little and accumulates skill. Each time the child accomplishes a little, he should be praised: "Good job." Since he already knows the piece through listening to the record frequently, the child can memorize it easily, which makes learning truly enjoyable for him.

ADVANCING TO BOOK 2

L EARNING by The Suzuki Method means never forgetting what is once learned, repeating it until it is thoroughly mastered, and thus developing fine ability. Therefore, teachers should guide students not to neglect playing the Book 1 pieces after they advance to Book 2. What wonderful ability it develops to play many pieces fluently without looking at the printed music is promptly understood once you try it yourself. In the traditional method of music education, little attention is paid to finished pieces. This fosters the failure to play fluently and cheerfully on the spot when asked to perform somewhere without time for practice.

The emphasis on producing good tone continues in Book 2. Even when children can listen to their own tone fairly well, distinguish between good and poor tone, and know how to play with good tone, when presented with slightly more difficult pieces, the children cannot do the same. Therefore, when advancing to a new piece, the teacher has to instruct in the same kindly and careful way: "If you play that note this way, you can easily produce a good tone!"

Daily home study must also continue. As the pieces become a little difficult on entering Book 2, parents who know little music begin to feel a bit anxious. Therefore the teacher must kindly and carefully instruct them in how to practice and improve difficult sections of a given piece. I try to give as concrete an assignment as possible. For example, I don't say "Prepare this part," but "Practice this part 20 times every day." Since listening to the record is more important than anything else, I also ask the parent at each lesson not to forget it.

The teacher must clearly distinguish between good and bad. Dr. Suzuki has written, "Don't scold children." Some misunderstand this (he said this because parents in the world scold all too frequently), and simply praise everything. This is a great mistake. If you only praise them, children come to take it for granted, and stop reacting. It's the same when you only scold them.

Children, unlike adults, are in a malleable period. If you let them hear both good tone and bad tone side by side, they understand the difference surprisingly well. When they promise to do an assignment, they understand clearly whether they have kept or not kept the promise. They also know whether they played well or not. The teacher must be honest with his students, and praise only the good.

Teachers must also continue to help their students to relax and to play naturally. This is not limited to the piano. In whatever activity, if any forcefulness exists, human beings tend to become so tense that the body becomes stiff and loses freedom.

Since the pieces become a little difficult after advancing to Book 2, please be careful so that the student does not hurry to the next piece when he cannot play the present one with sufficient fluency. Whether legato or staccato, take care that your students always play naturally as when walking. In case bad ability develops, the more advanced the student becomes, the more difficult it is to correct, and eventually it is impossible.

Reading Music

As I explained before, for children studying the piano, reading music is very important. I start reading when the child can play Book 1 skillfully and advances to Book 2. My method is the same whether the child is 3 or older. Any book is fine to use, but I choose a very easy book other than the Suzuki texts. The Suzuki texts are not suitable because they are familiar through the records and because Book 2 pieces are already fairly difficult.

First, I give the book to the child saying, "This is your reading book." It is the same as giving an illustrated book or fairy tale for the first time to a child who has turned 3- or 4-years old. Parents who have raised children know that children can't necessarily read it at once. First, they have to get used to the book.

I first teach the note of C in "Twinkle." Then I teach D, E, F, and G. Since this is The Suzuki Method, I ask the parent to repeat this every day at home. At the same time, I assign the child a one-hand piece of just a few measures to practice with the book on the piano music stand. The child can already play all of the Book 1 pieces, so this is an easy job. Children brought up on The Suzuki Method memorize the piece after playing it a few times.

It's fine for the child not to play with the eyes glued to the notes. Parents often misunderstand this. Since this is supposed to be reading, the parents tell their children, "You have to be looking at the music!" Please recall fairy tales. First the parents read them again and again to the child. Eventually the child memorizes the stories, and, vaguely looking at the printed letters, spontaneously learns to read.

I would like you to handle reading music in the same way. You should never rush, for children will end up hating it. However, never be lazy, either; create the time to practice reading a little at a time every day. The Suzuki principle is to foster ability. It means always to repeat every day; repeating the same thing is fine.

At this point, the student learns how to read the special signs in music, such as the crescendo. According to the traditional teaching method in music, the teacher gives instructions: "Crescendo there. Soft there! Accentuate that note!" A loyal student thinks he has to do it somehow, and tries playing the crescendo with all his might. When he succeeds, he is praised. When he goes home, he does not know how he did it right.

Please teach your students how to play and how to practice in order to get a crescendo effect or to produce other piano sounds. When I first observed Dr. Suzuki's lesson, I was struck to hear him say, "Play that section with very small bows," instead of "play it softly." Moved, I thought what a wonderful teaching method.

Conclusion

Instruction at the beginner stage depends solely on the teacher and the parent! The Suzuki Method considers every child at any moment has a wonderful potential. So we teachers must constantly try to give the highest advice to each child.

It is the same as in raising a child. Throughout the stages of growth from infancy to toddler's stage to childhood to adolescence, a good parent, I think, is always giving appropriate advice. And if it is loving and good advice, the child will become a fine, independent human being. It is exactly the same in piano education. In other words, it is an educational method which produces no dropouts. It is important to delight in and praise the child's progress, but if you don't watch out, bad habits may form before you know it. Until your child can firmly stand on his own feet, please guide him with deep love.

For the past several years, I have had opportunities for contact with parents not only in Japan but in several other countries. Although customs and manners may differ somewhat from country to country, parental love for children, I find, is a wonderful thing which is the same everywhere. Let's be better fathers, mothers, and teachers!